Confusion to Infusion

Remaining True in a Multi-Task World

Laura Hafford

PUBLISHER The Leaders Forge
www.ihimtv.com

ISBN: 9798666782057
e-book ISBN:

DEDICATION

I want to dedicate this book to my husband, who has been a strong tower against the opposition of those who say it can't be done. An example that when he sets his mind to doing something, he presses on unto completion.

Many thanks to Apostle's Matt and Amy Carpenter for encouraging me to get this started and for it reaching publication. You two are great examples of what we each can become when we walk in our identity in Christ.

Especially to those who read this book, who have been away from the Lord, and are searching for a re-connect with the Father. May you not lose but gain a foothold and keep climbing forward in intimate fellowship with Him.

Laura Hafford

CONTENTS

Why Do I Need to Read This Book?

It has been my experience growing up Jesus, that I have lapsed in my fellowship and even in my salvation. It was more a religious conversion. I found it necessary to not only come back to search and find the genuine relationship with my Heavenly Father that I was missing.

I did not find the path to enrich my time spent with the Lord that made it a fellowship with two-way communication. It resulted in a lot of wasted and empty years that I do not think is necessary when you find knowledge with Biblical reference to what you are going through. This knowledge may not catapult you but will redirect you into ways of connection with your Father God. A relationship that will produce joy and peace in all you do.

Laura Hafford

CHAPTER 1
IDENTIFY YOUR DESTINATION

What do you expect to gain from this book? In today's world, everything is competing for a piece of our twenty-four hours. How then do you create time to remain close to Christ and give yourself relational time with Him? It is important to make Christ a priority.

Matthew 6:33 says, "But seek ye first the kingdom of God, and his righteousness; and all these things shall be added unto you." (KJV)

What things will He add to you? This implies that if you surrender to living holy to the Lord that He will be faithful to you and care for you and your needs. Matthew 23:26 explains that we must first wash the inside of the cup and the dish, and thus the outside will become clean, too. This speaks of a pure heart, not outward performance.

There are dry seasons with the Lord. Some refer to these times as wilderness times, times of being hidden, or the black night of the soul. This may or may not have happened to you, but it set you in a place secluded from the Lord. Not that the Lord was not there with you, for it is His hope for you to perceive Him differently.

Graham Cooke states in his book, *Hiddeness & Manifestation,* this way, "In hiddenness and manifestation, being perplexed and learning to perceive things differently are key learning points." [1]

"You may have felt rejected by God as I did when I went through this. You may have felt deeply emotional because you could not feel or sense His presence with you. You may have felt void of any significance to your life as I did. Graham identifies other emotions felt in this time of hiddenness as; God has forgotten me, God has rejected me, God is angry with me, God is punishing me."[2]

It is God's desire not for you to pull away but to dig in. Hidden times is fundamental to develop your inner man in understanding things differently. It jolts you into looking to the deeper things of God. It helps you with character issues, wrong mindsets, and break down strongholds. These times allow God to purify your

---

[1] Cooke, Graham, *HIDDENNESS & MANIFESTATION* (Vancouver, WA, 2015), 31.
[2] Cooke, Graham, *HIDDENNESS & MANIFESTATION* (Vancouver, WA, 2015), 33-36.

motives and intentions. Holiness is an attitude of the heart. The result, if you pass through being hidden without stepping away from God, is you will have fresh insights ingrained upon your heart which transforms your mind to change your misconceptions to His Godly perspectives.

In Nehemiah (8:10) and Ezra's generation, they read the words of the law to the people, and they wept. Why? Because they realized they did not measure up to what the law ordered. Nehemiah and Ezra declared to them that this is not a moment to weep. It is a holy time and a moment of joy in the Lord that preserves you. It was not a time to dwell on their faults that convicted them, but to let their hearts be accessible to the Lord. To bring them joy by leading them and preparing them for the Lord. It is necessary to prove our motives, intentions, and our behaviors and make heart attitude adjustments. It is not for you to remain in a regretful demeanor and not step out to align yourself, but to be in relationship with the Lord. Great, if you have conviction of your lack of time spent with the one who made you for a relationship with Him. Don't stop there. Bring the joy of the Lord back into your spirit-man by fellowship with Father God. This is what these occasions produce.

Isaiah 55:3 reads, "Come to me with your ears wide open. Listen, and you will find life. I will make an everlasting covenant with you. I will give you all the unfailing love I promised to David." (NLT)

He promises to lavish his love, compassion, and forgiveness unto you when you turn to Him. Commit to not letting these valuable hours be a loss but invest in your relationship with the God who loves and cares all about you. He created you for fellowship with Him. The Holy Spirit will revive you.

John 17:17 says, "sanctify them through thy truth: thy word is truth." (KJV)

This transforms you in the heart and soul. It is necessary for the soul to transform, which will renew your mind.

Genesis 1:27 says that we're created in God's image. You have His abilities and the mind of Christ if you accept Him into your life. You cannot tolerate the hustle and bustle of everyday life and let it rob you of your fellowship with the Lord. This communion with the Father is absolutely what makes your day brighter and joyful, even in the worst of circumstances. Yes! I said that, even in the worst of circumstances. Remember that Paul was in chains in prison and wrote books of the Bible. Finding this kind of trust and hope in Christ is indeed what makes it an urgency to be in fellowship with Him daily.

Commit to blocking in a particular time each day to spend with your Heavenly Father. Today you are in a digital world. Therefore, it increases our options on audio bible readings or bible studies. It is an excellent tool because of its versatility in whatever occupation you work. If you are a housewife, you can turn it on and cook, clean, and take care of the kids. If you work in an office or have a distance to travel, you can listen to the word and have private time to commune.

Isaiah 54:1-14 reads,

11 "You unhappy one, storm-tossed and troubled, I am ready to rebuild you with precious stones and your intimacy with me will be built on a foundation of sapphires.

12 I will make your towers of rubies, your gates of sparkling jewels, and all your walls of precious, delightful stones.

13 All your children will be taught by Yahweh, and great will be their peace and prosperity.

14 You will be established in righteousness. Oppression—be far from you! (TPT)

Sapphire is a precious stone. They placed it in the second position of the priestly breastplate in the second row. It is described as extremely precious. The throne of God is like sapphire. It symbolizes wisdom, virtue, holiness, faithfulness, strength, and commitment. The sapphire is a foundation stone. You may be a sapphire that has not been laid open before God, but once you commit yourself to fellowship with the Lord, you will become a brilliant stone that is shining forth Christ! It is His promise spoken here to you; the one who is seeking for the Lord's comfort again.

It is for you to return and find the quiet time with the Lord to draw out what is precious. God planted it inside when He formed you. It is brought out and realized through your relationship with Him. Eventually, your foundation will reveal strength, faithfulness, and wisdom as you continue to be formed in righteousness. Be holy and commit to the Lord. Shine with what is polished and purified within you. You are the Bride of Christ who is radiant and loved immensely. Make sure your foundation stones are set upon the Lord.

Some of the most influential people I know start their day with the Lord before they do anything else. Why? You have the Word in you, and it is like eating a buffet that will sustain your spiritual strength throughout your day. My husband, an ex-military man, always says, "Failing to prepare yourself, is preparing yourself to fail." Prepare yourself by developing that ongoing relationship with the Lord.

1 John 4:4 reads, "You, dear children, are from God and have overcome them, because the one who is in you is greater than the one who is in the world." (NIV)

A sluggish and inconsistent relationship with the Lord is like the land Abraham accepted when he and Lot separated called Negev in Genesis thirteen. To look at this place, as Lot came to this conclusion, it was not a place you would want. It was desert like for most of the year, with very tiny springs and little rainfall. Animals could live there for a limited time. You can exist in the desert place for a brief time, but after that you might spiritually die.

Does this place have you craving for better? Then your Negev has been of some benefit. You may need to modify your destination.

Have you clarified your destination?

Have you fallen short of your destination?

Have you found that you are in a time of being hid and cannot find your course towards the Lord? If yes, can you now realize what you need to determine differently?

CHAPTER 2
ACCESS YOUR HELPER

Do you remember your first love? How good it felt to receive salvation. Consider how you feel now from how you felt then. Has complacency set in?

Complacency leads to no prayer life, no time spent in the Word, distractions, and no time with Jesus.

Isaiah 32:9-14 speaks of the complacent ones to rise.

> 9 "Rise up, you women who are at ease, hear my voice: you complacent daughters, give ear to my speech.
>
> 10 In little more than a year you will shudder, you complacent ones; for the grape harvest fails, the fruit harvest will not come.
>
> 11 Tremble, you women who are at ease, shudder, you complacent ones; strip, and make yourselves bare, and tie sackcloth around your waist.

12 Beat your breasts for the pleasant fields, for the fruitful vine,

13 for the soil of my people growing up in thorns and briers, yes, for all the joyous houses in the exultant city.

14a For the palace is forsaken, the populous city deserted...
ESV

The Lord's job is not to work out your holiness. It is up to you to seek repentance and to be holy as He is Holy. You may ask if this is contradicting what I have said in the previous chapter. No! There is a heart change that transforms your motives from receiver to obedience in service to your Lord. It culminates in outward holiness as He is Holy.

Jesus set you up to succeed by sending you the Comforter. The Holy Spirit is your champion, guide, and teacher to assist you. He helps you to navigate your life. He answers when you call out in your hour of need. As you are receptive to Him, you will receive from Him. He instills in you the same power that raised Christ from the dead.

Acts 1:8 reads, "But you will receive power and ability when the Holy Spirit comes upon you; and you will be My witnesses [to tell people about Me] both in Jerusalem and in all of Judea, and Samaria, and even to the ends of the earth." (AMP)

It is the power of the Holy Spirit that transform you to be like Jesus. You just need to be open to His guidance and be obedient.

What is holiness? It is righteous living, consecrated and set apart for God. Isaiah 63:4b reads, "… no eye has seen a God besides you, who acts for those who wait for him. 5a You meet him who joyfully works righteousness, those who remember you in your ways." It requires effort on your part to participate in living like Jesus and in your obedience, He will make available the help you need to be stable and grow further.

David was a man after God's own heart, but he was quick to relate to God his shortcomings, his anxiety, and his fears. In Psalm 6, David cries out to the Lord to deliver his life. It is the perfect place you need to run to switch your course from the 'highway of complacency' to the narrow road of righteous living.

The Holy Spirit in you makes living with a Kingdom mindset a reality. (Romans 14:17 TPT) The Holy Spirit brings you the joy, peace, and love needed for you to live the kingdom way.

Romans 8:14 reads, "For all who are led by the Spirit of God are sons of God." (NLT)

Cultivate righteousness like you would in a first-year garden. It takes constant attention to root out the bad weeds, thus revealing a yield of authentic beauty. I remember starting a new garden where the soil was so nice and rich. When I tilled that soil up, it automatically produced bad seeds that had to spring up. It was a battle to keep these thistles out of my garden. They were flourishing more than my precious vegetables were. I thought of spraying them with a chemical to combat their growth, but I didn't want those harsh chemicals affecting what I was producing.

This is like when you accepted the Lord in salvation and was immediately struck with opposition. Ways of the past try to replace your new found love of the Lord. Old friends that want to bring you back into their loop and do activities that do not cultivate growth you need. You must work hard to stay with your new love in the Lord.

Hebrews 6:1 says, "So let us stop going over the basic teachings about Christ again and again. Let us go on instead and become mature in our understanding. Surely we don't need to start again with the fundamental importance of repenting from evil deeds and placing our faith in God." (NLT)

Your trust must be in Christ Jesus.

1 Peter 2:2-3 reads, "Like newborn babies, crave pure spiritual milk, so that by it you may grow up in your salvation, 3 now that you have tasted that the Lord is good." (NLT)

Once you're saved the Holy Spirit is available to you to help you develop. The Holy Spirit acts like a parent showing you what to do and not to do through conviction.

Acts 5:32 reads, "And we are witnesses to these things, and so is the Holy Spirit, whom God has given to those who obey him."

Have you called upon the Holy Spirit to help you be consistent in reading, praying, and developing your relationship with Father God? You will need to take the first step in obedience.

How has the Holy Spirit been working in your life?

Have you sensed the Holy Spirit guiding you, bringing out truths, or encouraging you to be more responsive?

CHAPTER 3
STAY MOTIVATED

We all fall short in our walk with the Lord at times. The disciples, as close as they were with Jesus, scattered after Jesus was arrested and taken from them. They each had to come back into focus and alignment with the Lord. What brought them back? The Holy Spirit and I believe that it was their love for Jesus. They failed to stand by Him, but the important point is they renewed their fellowship with Him. Jesus in return did not condemn them but took that move in His direction and gave them instruction, love, and knowledge that He would be there for them always. This is grace.

Jesus knows your weakness, and He desires for you to return to Him and realign your life in relationship with Him. Is it necessary for you to fall away from the Lord when you are weak confronting your trials, strongholds, and problems? No. He is always there for you. You just need to stay close to Him in fellowship and He will instruct you, encourage you, and guide you with the Holy Spirit.

Like any relationship you have, be diligent in staying connected to it. What motivates this relationship? You don't want to slacken. You want to keep involved and engaged constantly. Otherwise you will have to repeat what ground you have covered.

When I was a young girl about nine years old, the Lord showed me a vision of himself. I was the middle child with a brother and sister older than me and a brother and sister younger than me. I have no recollection of what had me discouraged that day. In that old Rambler car, we were all squished into it with my parents. God met me there. I was sitting by the window. I looked up to the full moon, and Jesus was in it. I was astonished! I wondered, am "I really seeing this?" I wanted to tell my siblings but didn't want to look away. It mesmerized me. I watched and then looked at my siblings to see if they were seeing Him too. When I looked back, He was gone. That vision of Jesus sustained me for many years that He is there, and he picked me to show himself to.

The Lord is faithful and loving towards you. He wants you to make time for Him to tell you and show you things that will amaze you. It will grow you up into your true identity in Him and accomplish superb feats for the kingdom.

Ephesians 5:26, 27 says, "That he might sanctify and cleanse it with the washing of water by the word, that he might present it to himself a glorious church, not having spot, or wrinkle, or any such thing; but that it should be holy and without blemish."(NKJV)

Sanctification by definition is to be set apart as or declare holy; consecrate, free from sin, purify, cause to be or seem morally right or acceptable. To be sanctified you need to have a relationship with the one who can purify your soul and walk in union with the Almighty daily. When you set yourself apart for the Lord, you can align with the guidance of the Holy Spirit. The Word of God continually transforms you in the likeness of Jesus. It is a continual process, and that is why the Bible says we are transformed from glory to glory (2 Corinthians 3:18). An active prayer life is very much a part of your sanctification. If you continue to strive towards sanctification or holiness, you are a benefit of God's blessings on others.

1 Thessalonians 5:23 reads, "May God himself, the God who makes everything holy and whole, make you holy and whole, put you together—spirit, soul, and body—and keep you fit for the coming of our Master, Jesus Christ. The One who called you is completely dependable. If he said it, he'll do it!" (MSG)

Do not remain in a state of a guilty conscience.

John 10:9,10 reads, "I am the door. If anyone enters by Me, he will be saved, and will go in and out and find pasture. The thief does not come except to steal, and to kill, and to destroy. I have come that they may have life, and that they may have it more abundantly." (NKJV)

Jesus is always ready to receive anyone who comes to Him. Verse nine says that he will go in and out; and find pasture. Does that mean that you will go in and out of Christ? I believe that He meant for you to find Him in all your situations. Whether you are busy, under stress, in conflict with others. You can find Him in any of your situations if you rest in His peace in all things.

Matthew 19:26 says, "But Jesus looked at them and said, 'With man this is impossible, but with God all things are possible." (ESV)

In 1 Corinthians 15:58 he says that we don't strive in vain. There is a purpose to your sacrifice of time with Him. That purpose is an abundant and fulfilled life because you found your true identity in Christ. This is fulfilling.

2 Corinthians 12:9 says, "But he said to me, 'My grace is sufficient for you, for my power is made perfect in weakness. Therefore I will boast all the more gladly of my weaknesses, so that the power of Christ may rest upon me." (ESV)

Paul knew how to find his true north with all his ins and outs. He could find rest or peace of mind because He knew Jesus that intimately. Paul could find green pasture wherever and whatever he found himself in.

CHAPTER 4
TAKE ACTION

Isaiah 56:1-8 speaks of how the Lord accepts those who have been longing for this relationship with Him. He exhorts those that are outside of the faith to come and join him. He promises you that instead of being displaced you will have honor, favor, blessing, and full of joy.

The action from you that is required is to accept Him as Lord, honor Jesus, and keep the core values of righteous living-cultivate righteousness, love Him above all others and other things, and to worship Him in prayer and thanksgiving. This denotes that you keep a healthy flourishing relationship with Him daily. Commit to being obedient.

Why does Jesus do this? He loves you. It is His motive. He would not have sacrificed Himself without this great love for you. He did it for you.

Psalm 23:1-3, The Lord is my best friend and my shepherd.2. I always have more than enough.3. He offers a resting place for me in his luxurious love.

His tracks take me to an oasis of peace, the quiet brook of bliss.

That is where He restores and revives my life.

He opens before me pathways to God's pleasure

And leads me along in His footsteps of righteousness

So that I can bring honor to His name. (TPT)

Recently I went to Brazil to visit some former foreign students that stayed with us on their college breaks. I was overwhelmed with the love that God lavished on me while in Brazil. God had preordained this trip to instill in me his great love for me and reinforce the call he has on my life. People who didn't even know me poured into my life with gifts, food, prophetic words, and encouragement.

Father God cares about you. He has a calling for you. He has given you gifts for the kingdom. No one else can use those gifts like He gave you to use. Father wants you to be encouraged. By reading the Word and communing with Him, you will be more relaxed and at peace throughout your busy day. It is the very answer to what you are searching for.

Hebrews 4:16, "So let us come boldly to the throne of our gracious God. There we will receive his mercy, and we will find grace to help us when we need it most." (NLT)

You can find this fellowship with Him if you persevere, fully trusting Him that He will be there with you.

James 4:8 says it this way, "Come close to God, and God will come close to you. Wash your hands, you sinners; purify your hearts, for your loyalty is divided between God and the world." (NLT)

The people in Colossae had a similar problem. Paul addressed a problem that they loved to learn, but they didn't consider the misleading information they were receiving. Colossae was once a thriving city but was bypassed by the populous in later time because of rerouting of roads, much like a by-pass would do around cities. This may have influenced the Colossians to want to grasp onto this misleading teaching to give them influence.

The second problem Paul addressed with them was that they were not growing up to live in the way Jesus taught. It is for you to read the Word and apply it to your everyday life. The Colossians were mixing this dangerous doctrine in with the truth of the Word. They showed love, but no growth. People who stay in the "milk" level too long may not understand the love that God has for them.

2 Peter 1:5-8says, "For this very reason, make every effort to supplement your faith with virtue, and virtue with knowledge, and knowledge with self-control, and self-control with steadfastness, and steadfastness with godliness, and godliness with brotherly affection, and brotherly affection with love. For if these qualities are yours and are increasing, they keep you from being ineffective or unfruitful in the knowledge of our Lord Jesus Christ." (ESV)

It is imperative to study the Word and let it transform your life.

Ephesians 2:10, "For we are his workmanship, created in Christ Jesus for good works, which God prepared beforehand, that we should walk in them." (ESV)

If you are not walking in God's footsteps you are walking in the enemy's path. There is no lukewarm. Either you choose to, or you choose not to work out your salvation. Either you make the commitment to have a daily relationship with Father or you don't.

In **Acts 14:22** Paul encourages us to go deeper in our faith: "strengthening the souls of the disciples, exhorting them to continue in the faith, and saying, 'We must through many tribulations to **enter the kingdom** of God." (NKJV)

You have heard that "anything that is easy, isn't worth having". You place greater value and cherish things more when you have poured yourself into something.

CHAPTER 5
WHAT IS THE SECRET PLACE?

What is this secret place? It is the place that you come into alone, into His Presence. A place where everything else is put aside, and it is just you and Him. But how can you find this place?

Paul formerly called Saul before he found this secret place. He was hell bent on destroying all these Jesus freaks. His life was completely devoted to being under the law. Because of this lifestyle, Saul built up a life devoid of true Christian character and theology. It was revealed to him at his miraculous conversion. Now called "Paul" and scribed the epistles including

1 Corinthians 3:15. It reads, "If any man's work shall be burned, he shall suffer loss: but he himself shall be saved; yet so as by fire." (KJV)

1 Corinthians chapter 3 further shows that Paul

understood that it's not about us but the transformation that takes place within us. You are part of the big picture, and it is the Lord who grows you. What remains when you stand before Him will be the key. This development is between you and the Lord, with the Holy Spirit's efficient help.

Psalm 27:5 reads, "In his shelter in the day of trouble, that's where you'll find me, for he hides me there in his holiness. He has smuggled me into his secret place, out of reach from all my enemies." (TPT)

It's a place that you commune with Him. David knew it was his God that made him shine so that the surrounding people recognized it. Here is a hidden secret place David speaks of that not only was he protected by God, but this place produced growth in him that others also realized and looked to him for guidance and courage from it.

Matthew Henry Commentary explains it this way, "The gracious presence of God, His power, His promise, His readiness to hear prayer, the witness of His Spirit in the hearts of His people-these are the secret of His tabernacle, and in these the saints find cause for that holy security and serenity of mind in which they dwell at ease." This secret place is where change has to occur when you are diligent enough to seek it out, your heart is ready for transformation.

What do you get from this secret place? In the secret place you first give God honor. You sacrifice your time and desperately seek to find this allotted time to be with Him. You give Him your heartfelt gratitude and thankfulness for being a relational God. It is of desiring this intimacy with Him that you separate yourself. We then receive from the secret place joy, goodness, and an integrity from being transformed from time spent in His presence.

Psalm 91:1 says, "He that dwells in the secret place of the most high shall abide under the shadow of the Almighty," (KJV).

You get fresh perspectives that are in line with a kingdom mentality. It results in even more manifestation of God in you.

John 14:21 reads, "Those who truly love me are those who obey my commands. Whoever passionately loves me will be passionately loved by my Father. And I will passionately love you in return and will manifest my life within you." (TPT)

Things like the fruit of the Spirit: love, joy, peace, patience, kindness, goodness, faithfulness, gentleness, and self-control that Galatians 5:22-23 speaks of. It is a place where you know, are sure of, God's great love for you. It is a place that you find revelation. It is the place that you have the faith to believe in the great promises He has spoken to you specifically. You will have confidence in walking them out because you see them as truth.

In the secret place you will find God's Presence because you have yielded to Him. This attracts His Presence to you. It is this depth of knowing God is your all in all, and your desire is deeply searching for more and more of Him. A sense of awe rises from within you as you show adoration to God Almighty.

Have you found the secret place with the Lord?

How will you make your first step in setting this time for the Lord?

CHAPTER 6
CONNECT IN PRAYER

Sometimes when you have been absent from relationship with the Lord, you find it hard to pray. It feels mechanical and unfeeling. You undoubtedly feel the disconnect. It's all right, He is still there, and He is waiting to talk with you. Just like the prodigal son returning home, it overjoys him for your return. Just talk to Him and repent of your lapse no matter what the reason was. Let your spirit witness with the Holy Spirit in communion with Him.

Graham Cooke and Allison Bown's CD series of *PRAYING WITH GOD,* [3] introduce you two ways to enter prayer. They teach you that it is vital to come into prayer and be still before the Lord and to just absorb His

---

[3] Cooke, Graham and Bown, Allison. (2019). *PRAYING WITH GOD*. Brilliant Book House.

presence. The gap between asking and hearing generally is about being filled with His Presence. Graham says, "that prayer becomes a relational place where we abide, listen, and receive the provision that God has already made for us."

1 Timothy 2:8 reads, "Therefore, I encourage the men to pray on every occasion with hands lifted to God in worship with clean hearts, free from frustration or strife." (TPT) This scripture also points to making a heart adjustment when we come before the Father in prayer.

To use Jesus' example in **Mark 1:35,** "And rising very early in the morning, while it was still dark, he departed and went out to a desolate place, and there he prayed." (ESV)

This early morning time of prayer is the most relational time to be with the Lord for me. It is that peacefulness of nothing else going on around me; no vehicles, no television, or other technical devices, no one who needs my attention. It's just me and the Lord.

There have been other times in my life that His presence has showed up in big ways. A lesson of this was while at camp by myself, devoting more time to studying the Word and praying in depth. I remember going to bed and God's presence just descended around me like a cloud. It felt so thick and beautiful. He just bathed me in His presence it may have not been for exceptionally long, but for me, time seemed to stand still. At first, I said nothing, and Father didn't either. I just enjoyed His presence so much. It was like the scripture that talks of His wrap around Presence. You will not always feel His Presence like this. It is a walk of faith.

You must believe He is there with you. After a time, I talked with Him. It is a great joy to have that closeness, that fellowship with the Almighty. You don't always feel His presence like this, but you need to know that He is there and listening to you. His very name, Immanuel, means 'God is with us.'

Isaiah 41:10 says, "Do not fear [anything], for I am with you; Do not be afraid, for I am your God. I will strengthen you, be assured I will help you; I will certainly take hold of you with My righteous right hand [a hand of justice, of power, of victory, of salvation]." (AMP)

Whether or not you feel you are connecting with Him, He is still with you. This is the dispensation of grace, and that will not change until judgement day. His grace covers us and He is always with us. Nothing can keep us from Him.

Matthew 18:20 says, "For where two or three are gathered in my name, there am I among them." (ESV)

Does this mean that there must be at least two for Him to be there with you? No. **Matthew 28:20** says, "… and surely I am with you always, to the very end of the age." (NIV) He is with you. He will hear you.

Your approach in prayer is to be one of thankfulness and worship. You have so much to be thankful for every day. The Lord wants to hear you express your thankfulness to Him. To give the glory and honor that He so deserves.

It does not mean you come to Him in prayer with constant petitions, but you also tell Him how thankful you are for all that He is and done for you. Worship is the expression resulting from your heart in tune with His. To worship Him in spirit and in truth means that He is omnipresent. You do not have to be in a church to worship Him. He is always with you. It is not a ritual or a religious act, but it is a heart of love towards the Lord. It is heartfelt. It's your spirit man in touch with the Spirit of God.

Pawendtare Kombassare, a pastor, teacher, and humble man of God, once said that "prayer is the connection that feeds us the strength to do whatever work we have to do." Jesus gave us many examples of how to pray. Prayer connects us to our heavenly source (Matthew 14:23). He taught us to pray, to increase our faith, to increase our compassion and trust in God. To give us strength (Psalm 138:3), to bring peace to our hearts and minds (Philippians 4:6,7) and to show us the will of God in our decision making (Matthew 26:39, Luke 6:12,13).

Not merely did Jesus teach us how to pray, but He is still praying and interceding for us today.

Hebrews 7:25 says, "Therefore He is also able to save to the uttermost those who come to God through Him, since He always lives to make intercession for them." (NKJV)

His love for you did not stop at the cross. He wants you to succeed in Kingdom living through your Kingdom connection of prayer.

Do you realize how important it is to have a consistent prayer life?

Do you hear God speaking to you when you pray? If not, spend more time meditating and freeing your heart up to Him.

How does your prayer life affect you?

How does Jesus' example of praying help you pray?

CHAPTER 7
DIGEST THE WORD

Deuteronomy 4:29 reads, "But from there you will seek the Lord your God and you will find Him, if you search after Him with all your heart and with all your soul." (ESV)

Make your spiritual relationship with Him a priority. Don't focus on your circumstances but concentrate on your goal of restoring your life with the Lord. Have faith that you can do this.

Psalm 32:8 says, "I will instruct you and **teach you** in the way you should go; I will counsel you with my eye upon you." (ESV)

For this to take effect it will take you to be attentive in reading the Word which will produce truth to you.

Matthew 12:20 says, "a bruised reed he will not break, and a smoldering wick he will not quench, until he brings justice to victory;" (ESV).

You may have struggled to re-establish fellowship with the Lord. But in this verse, it reveals to us that you still have time to start. His grace is even present until the day of judgement. He loves you even when you haven't "trimmed your wick". He is ready and watching you to illuminate you with His Word.

I can sum this up in these scriptures found in **Proverbs 2:1-12**, "My son, if you receive my words and treasure up my commandments with you, 2 **making your ear attentive** to wisdom and inclining your heart to understanding; 3 yes, if you call out for insight and raise your voice for understanding, 4 if you seek it like silver and search for it as for hidden treasures, 5 then you will understand **the fear of the Lord** and find the knowledge of God. 6 For the Lord gives wisdom; from his mouth come knowledge and understanding; 7 he stores up sound wisdom for the upright; he is a shield to those who walk in integrity, 8 guarding the paths of justice and watching over the way of his saints. 9 Then you will understand righteousness and justice and equity, every good path; 10 for **wisdom will come into your heart**, and knowledge will be pleasant to your soul; 11 **discretion** will watch over you, **understanding** will guard you, 12 delivering you from the way of evil," (ESV).

Jeremiah 15:16 says, "Your words were found, and I ate them, and your words became to me a joy and the delight of my heart, for I am called by your name, O Lord, God of hosts." (ESV)

You cannot simply be listeners of the Word but digest it and let it transform your life.

James 1:25 reads, "But the one who looks into the perfect law, the law of liberty, and perseveres, being no hearer who forgets but a doer who acts, he will be blessed in his doing." (ESV)

Reading the Word reveals truths to your spirit man and helps transform you.

John 16:15 says, "Everything that belongs to the Father belongs to me-that's why I say that the Divine Encourager will receive what is mine and reveal it to you." (TPT)

The Holy Spirit helps you out in the transformation area. You consistently need transformation. It's a process that is ongoing and Father approved.

Having a fear of the Lord in your Christian life is of significant benefit:

- It will bring you joy and gladness.
- It will spare you of pain and suffering.
- It leads to abundant life. Proverbs 14:27.
- It gives us great confidence. Proverbs 14:26.
- It gives us friendship with the Lord. Proverbs 25:14.
- It motivates us to worship God and follow hard after Him.

Reading the Bible and meditating on what is written will become a part of you.

Joshua 1:8 says, "This book of the law shall not depart out of your mouth; but you shall meditate therein day and night, that you may observe to do according to all that is written therein: for then you shall make your way prosperous, and then you shall have good success." (KJV)

It doesn't mean you will be wealthy in the sense of having lots of money, but that you will have the wealth of God's Word in you and walk in its truth.

Romans 10:17 reiterates what we receive from meditating on the Word: "So faith comes from hearing, and hearing through the word of Christ." (ESV)

It expands your faith in the Lord. You learn to trust more and more in Him. Relying on Him to be present consistently. When given opportunity you express it to people that are in your sphere of influence. It then shapes them.

Hebrews 4:12 reads, "For we have the living Word of God, which is full of energy, and it pierces more sharply than a two-edged sword. It will even penetrate to the very core of our being where soul and spirit, bone and marrow meet! It interprets and reveals the true thoughts and secret motives of our hearts." (TPT)

That is exceptional! It will influence you!

CHAPTER 8
NEW BEGINNINGS

I ended this book with eight chapters because eight signifies new beginnings. So, by now you have a starting point. There is not one whom the Lord cannot use. Let me give you some examples:

Kris Vallotton-was a mechanic who never attended college—now has authored multiple revelatory books to help others and is a leader in a mega-church.

Corrie Ten Boone-Born in near poverty, was a prisoner to an evil dictator in a situation that looked hopeless—her life spared. She authored books and has a powerful legacy of faith that remains to encourage others.

Graham Cooke-once imprisoned—now is a writer, pastor, and prophetic teacher and touching thousands of people in showing who the one true God is.

All these people had new beginnings. They did not allow their dire circumstances to derail them permanently. They found the Truth with new, transformed expressions of who they truly are in Christ. What is your present priority keeping you from becoming what your Father in heaven sees? How much greatness is there still hiding in you? Why won't you take a step in the Father's direction and apply daily to discovering your hidden potential?

Psalm 33:4 reminds us that the Lord is faithful. The Lord will be faithful to keep His promises to you. Faithful in His promise for Holy Spirit to counsel you, guide you, help you, teach you, pray and intercede for you.

So now you are down to it. Have you formulated your 'stick-to-it' plan?

Have you identified areas that can be a pitfall to you? During this, have you improved your manner of avoiding these same traps?

Prioritize it. Set a schedule and stick to it. As I am writing this, people across the globe are talking about "what is essential" during a pandemic. Prioritizing your personal devotional bible study and personal time spent with the Lord are essential to your life in Christ.

Keys to success:

Pick a devotional, prayer and rest time and practice keeping it for the next 6 months.

Hebrews 11:6 reads, "And without faith it is impossible to please him, for whoever would draw near to God must believe that he exists and that he rewards those that seek him." (ESV)

Be constant and attentive to reaching your goal of fellowship with your Lord and Savior.

Be expectant and confident to see growth in the Lord and where He will bring you. Compromise your diligence in fellowship with the Lord will jeopardize and derail your future commitment to a daily walk.

There are many devotional aides to assist you in understanding and that you may find promote your time in study. Commentaries, different versions of the Bible and Bible studies. We can find them on CD's, MP3, eBooks, or paperback to keep you on track and faithful. Many books are helpful in reinforcing what you need to establish fellowship with the Lord.

Pray and ask the Lord now to show you a path forward. Expect to see His hand guiding you. It will attract Him, and He will guide you as you keep searching for Him.

I will encourage you with this scripture from **Psalm 37:4-7:** "Take delight in the Lord and He will give you the desires of your heart. Commit your way to the Lord; trust in Him and He will do this: He will make your righteous reward shine like the dawn, your vindication like the noonday sun. Be still before the Lord and wait patiently for Him." (NIV) I commend you for your desire to take up your cross and follow after Him. Ephesians 3:20 reads, "Now all glory to God, who is able, through his mighty power at work within us, to accomplish infinitely more than we might ask or think." (NLT)

A PRAYER FOR YOU

I pray Christ has made you His own, and that you press on, forgetting what is past and beginning anew. I pray that you continue steadfast in your prayer life with thanksgiving, and that in your devotional life you find the mystery of Christ. I pray that you walk in a new-found wisdom and make the best use of your time. I pray you will grow well seasoned in the Word. That you display it without thought to others. May your heart connection with Jesus radiate through you to the world around you. I pray that you can envision Christ's smiling face upon you because you please Him. Be devote in holiness. Remembering that Christ is for you and not against you.

ABOUT THE AUTHOR

Laura is a compassionate leader and woman of God who desires to see others find true fellowship with God the Father.

Laura Attended 2 years at Zion Bible Institute. She is an ordained minister through John Hunter Ministries. A Graduate from Northern Maine Community College as a registered nurse.

She is a former VBS Director, Youth Leader, and Worshiper. She has awards in 4 Corner Alliance Member.

Laura is a speaker/teacher on "The Way of Holiness". She carries in her ministry and life a prophetic calling, stalwart mercy, and a healing anointing.

She lives in Northern Maine with her husband Calvin.